Expanding the

BORDERS

of your

EXPECTATION

God Has More for You!

GARY WARD

WESTBOW
PRESS®
A DIVISION OF THOMAS NELSON
& ZONDERVAN

Scripture taken from the NEW AMERICAN STANDARD BIBLE®,
Copyright © 1960,1962,1963,1968,1971,1972,1973,1975,1977,
1995 by The Lockman Foundation. Used by permission

WestBow Press books may be ordered through
booksellers or by contacting:

WestBow Press
A Division of Thomas Nelson & Zondervan
1663 Liberty Drive
Bloomington, IN 47403
www.westbowpress.com
1 (866) 928-1240

ISBN: 978-1-5127-7266-1 (sc)
ISBN: 978-1-5127-7268-5 (hc)
ISBN: 978-1-5127-7267-8 (e)

Library of Congress Control Number: 2017900877

Print information available on the last page.

WestBow Press rev. date: 01/23/2017

Contents

Introduction

We need a spiritual revival. If you agree, this book is for you. It is designed to present a perspective that may be different than what you are used to.

There seem to be two major viewpoints regarding a coming revival and whether or not we have a part in bringing it about. One is that if we just develop enough programs, get enough people involved in doing things and pray enough, revival will come. The other view is that God is sovereign; He will do whatever He wants to do and when He wants to do it.

There is another view that is somewhere between those two extremes. That is, we can provide an environment—or atmosphere—of faith and expectation that will allow the Holy Spirit an opportunity to move as He wills.

Along with this view, it is important to note that God is creative, and He has various effective ways to carry out His plans and purposes. He does not want to be restrained by our putting Him in a box. He does not need a five-step plan or some formula that must be followed in order to manifest Himself.

You may never have experienced a miracle from God. Or you may have experienced many wondrous works from Him. The major point of this book is to encourage you that, no matter where you are with your own experiences, no matter how greatly the Lord has or has not moved in your life—God has much more for you and your church!

The exciting testimonies included in the pages to follow are to encourage you and to motivate you to expand the borders of your expectation! But first let us take a brief look at the Apostle Paul's perspective.

Chapter 1

Paul's Perspective

God was performing extraordinary miracles
by the hands of Paul, so that handkerchiefs
or aprons were even carried from his body
to the sick, and the diseases left them and
the evil spirits went out. (Acts 19:11–12)

Paul had come to Ephesus, found some disciples, and asked them if they had received the Holy Spirit. Their reply was that they had not even heard of the Holy Spirit. After he prayed for them and they received the Holy Spirit, God showed them and others that there was much more He had for them.

There is more that God has for all of us.

Paul said, "Not that I have already obtained it or have already become perfect, but I press on so that I may lay hold of that for which also I was laid hold of by Christ Jesus" (Philippians 3:12).

Paul carried such an anointing that even handkerchiefs and aprons from his body brought healing to the sick and deliverance to those harassed or inhabited by demons. Nevertheless, he said he knew there were more things of God that he had yet to understand and experience.

If you or your church are exceeding the works that God did through Paul, then perhaps you might as well stop reading any farther. This book is written for those who acknowledge that, no matter how many signs, wonders, and miracles they have experienced, there is more. We need to expand the borders of our expectation.

We can learn at least two things from Paul. First, he fully realized there is much more God would like to do in us and through us. Second, he realized that expectation can be a limiting or enhancing factor in receiving more from the Lord.

Speaking of his imprisonment, he said, "I know that this will turn out for my deliverance through your prayers and the provision of the Spirit of Jesus Christ, according to my earnest expectation and hope.... " (Philippians 1:19–20).

Included in the three things he said would be important in his deliverance was his "earnest expectation."

This book is designed to encourage you, as an individual and as a church congregation, that much more awaits you, and that your faith and expectation have a lot to do with whether or not, and how much of it, you receive.

Paul said that he was "pressing on" with "earnest expectation." Earnest expectation is defined as *strained* expectation. It implies confidence and assurance.

That almost sounds akin to faith, doesn't it? "Now faith is the assurance of things hoped for, the conviction of things not yet seen" (Hebrews 11:1).

Real Bible faith is beyond just believing that God's Word is true. When you come to the place where you know God's Word is true, you press on toward it with strained anticipation. You expand the boundaries of your expectation.

As you read this book, I want you to be encouraged by the testimonies and principles—all based on God's Word. And I pray that, no matter how many wonderful things you have experienced with the Lord, you will know that there are more!

Chapter 2

Despise Not Small Beginnings

No matter how many wonderful and amazing things you have experienced and learned, they are yet small in terms of all that God has for us.

In the fourth chapter of Zechariah we read the account of an angel who appeared to the prophet and showed him things in the spiritual realm. He asked Zechariah if he knew what they were. The answer was, no. The angel then showed him more things and inquired whether or not he knew what they were. The same answer: no.

In the tenth verse the angel made this statement: "For who has despised the day of small things?" As you read on, the angel was clearly showing Zechariah that you ain't seen nothin' yet. That was my paraphrase to get your attention! But the point is that there is more to come no matter how many revelations, visions, signs and wonders we have seen.

If we wanted to use further, more contemporary expressions, we might say that what we have experienced with God is only the tip of the iceberg, or that we have only scratched the surface. So you may have experienced big things with God, but they are small in comparison to what He has for us.

As we expand our borders of expectation, be sure they expand in areas that are in agreement with God's Word, the Bible. If it is not in His Word, leave it alone. If it is, go for it.

The starting point is wherever we are. We go from where we are and continue to learn more about, and experience more of, the things of God in our individual lives and in our churches.

Stay on the Word, but do not hesitate to step out—to press on—even when you face situations you have never faced before.

In nearly forty years of ministry, both before and in the pastorate, my wife and I have seen many remarkable works of God. I will be sharing some to encourage you. If you continue to press on and expand the borders of your faith and expectation, someday you may write your own book and leave a legacy of faith to pass on to others to encourage them.

The Beginning

Let's take a look to see how God can move through us as we only begin. Years ago, before being called into full-time ministry, my wife and I were members of a church that did not believe in healing. I am assuming they didn't. They never talked about it. If you really believe in something, don't you talk about it?

We began to study God's Word, attend meetings with other believers, and learn from some friends who were more mature in their faith, and we were seeing some healings which encouraged us to press in and learn more.

After observing two people who received healings for very painful and serious back problems, Carolyn said to me, "I think you should go over and offer to pray for Larry. I heard he is having great problems with his back."

I did not want to go. I didn't have any experience in doing that kind of thing. That would be new territory for me. It was beyond the borders of my current expectation. We had seen in the Bible how Jesus healed people, but I thought I just wasn't ready for that.

After her really persistent insistence that I go, I went. I found his house, walked up to the door and knocked lightly. After all, if he were napping, I didn't want to wake him, or so I rationalized.

After a slightly louder knock and no one came to the door, I thought I was free to return home and report that I tried, but it didn't work out. No one was home.

Then I noticed the doorbell and realized if I didn't try that, I could be in trouble. But no one came to the door.

Okay. I tried all I could. I didn't think I should have made the trip here in the first place. I wasn't ready for this.

I got in the car and began to drive away, and somehow I "heard" this: "Go around the block and turn down the alley." It came to me a second time and I ignored it, but the third time I wheeled around and drove down the alley.

You are probably ahead of me on this. That's right. Larry was in his back yard near the alley. He saw me, so I had to stop. I somehow managed to tell him about the back healings we had seen, and I offered to pray for him.

When we went inside, I had him sit on a straight chair, and I found myself asking him if he happened to have one leg shorter than the other. He replied, "Oh yes. I have to wear a big lift in the shoe on the shorter leg."

I reached down, took hold of his feet, and began to pray. "In Jesus' name...." I don't remember what else I prayed, but after only a minute or so I heard crying. In those days I thought when you prayed you had to close your eyes. I learned later you can pray with eyes wide open and watch what God is doing.

His wife was crying, and I asked her what was going on. She replied that, as I began to pray, she saw her husband's short leg grow out.

I asked him what was gong on. He said, "When you began to pray, I literally felt something come upon me at the top of my head. It washed down through my body, and when it went out my shorter leg, I felt it grow." Then, with heavy tears, he said repeatedly, "I have never felt so clean in all my life!"

It was only later I learned that Larry had been an alcoholic, and as the Spirit of God washed him clean, He not only healed Larry's leg and his back problems, but also delivered him from the addiction of alcoholism he had dealt with for years. Glory to God!

Now why did I share all that in such detail? So that you might see that, no matter where you perceive yourself to be spiritually, if you will step out and just do what is in accordance with God's Word, He will perform the Word according to His promises and provisions.

Do you think my faith level increased after that? Do you think after that I expanded my borders of expectation of what God can do in us, with us, and through us—all for His glory? I sure did, and I intend to continue to do so.

Despise not what might seem like a small beginning. Step out. Press in.

Are you up to one more small-beginnings story? If so, the next chapter has another one. Then we will move on and expand it out much further than my experiences. I'm just trying to show you how I have experienced what I am trying to encourage you in—expanding your borders of faith and expectation.

Chapter 3

The Starting Point Is Wherever You Are

Before being called into full-time ministry, I was teaching biology at our local high school. It was then that we got a phone call late at night. The person on the other end was garbled in speech. I tried to communicate to no avail.

I thought this might be a prank call from a student. But Carolyn had picked up the extension phone, and she discerned a problem. I told the caller I was ready to hang up if she would not speak in a way I could understand.

Carolyn came flying down the stairs and told me, "Don't hang up. Keep talking. Keep the woman on the line!" She ran out the door looking for a neighbor's house with lights still on late at night. (This was before cell phones.) She found a house down the street, and from there, called the police. She explained that there was a potential problem, and she asked if they could trace the call and send an officer to investigate. It was a long shot, but she felt it was worth a try.

In the meantime, someone walked into the room of the caller and said something that gave me a clue as to who it was.

We drove to the woman's house. There we discovered that she was in a very drunken state. She was disheveled, nose running, hair all messed up, and crying.

A police car arrived shortly, and Carolyn went out to talk with the officer to explain that we were there to help, and the officer was glad to let us do it.

Meanwhile, I took the woman, put my hands on her shoulders, held her up on her feet and commanded, "In Jesus' name, you spirit of alcoholism, come out of her. Depart and never return!"

At that point, I realized that was as far as I had learned about casting out demons, so I let her go and she fell to the floor.

Carolyn came back in, sat on the floor with the woman, and told her that we loved her and that God loves her, too.

The next day the woman called and said she could remember only one thing from the night before. That was that someone put her arms around her in her disheveled state and told her that God loves her. Love abides.

Later we learned two other things. She was delivered that night from her alcoholism, and we found out how it happened that she called us. She was trying to dial a friend whose phone number had the same numbers as ours, but in a different order. She made a God-ordained "mistake." In her condition she mis-dialed the number. She was trying to call her friend to tell her that she was going to kill herself that night.

At that time I was just learning about the authority Jesus gave us over demons and that He had instructed His followers to cast them out. The point of this story is to encourage you to keep learning God's Word, step out, and do what you have learned to do in accordance with His Word. He will honor that effort and move through you in mighty ways to help others.

Know that you have not yet attained it all; but press on. Expand the borders of your expectation.

These two stories were to help you see that, even though you may not have all the answers, and you don't understand some things, the Lord will make up the difference if you sincerely keep pressing on, learning more, and expanding the borders of your expectations.

Chapter 4

The Importance of Practice

Most people understand that practice makes us better. Remember the first time you shot a basketball at a goal? Swoosh! It went right in, right? Probably not. Maybe not even the second or third or.....?

If you learned how to play a musical instrument as a child, your parents probably still remember what it sounded like at first.

Do you know why you probably did not go on to be a collegiate basketball player or to play a musical instrument like the musician you most admire? Mostly because you did not think it was important enough to invest the time and energy into practicing. You were not willing to practice for hours each day to become proficient.

Is that the way it is with some Christians? It is not important enough to invest the effort to become more efficient and proficient in being used in mighty ways by the Lord?

Spending time in the Word of God, spending time in prayer with Him, learning and doing what the Word says to do—Is it just not worth the effort, when compared to all the other things going on in your life?

How Complicated Is It?

As you personally, or as your church makes a decision to expand your borders of expectation, how difficult is it? How many hours or years do you have to study the Word? Closely follow the Scriptures below. They will be an indication of how complicated it needs to be.

> Every word of God is true (tested, flawless). He is a shield to those who take refuge in Him. Do not add to His words or He will reprove you and you will be proved a liar. (Proverbs 30:5)

You must believe God's Word is true. Do not add to it. How do we add to it? With conjunctions. Remember in grammar class where you learned about conjunctions and how they join two opposing thoughts together?

You add to God's Word with conjunctions, and in doing so, you negate the Word. Example: You say, "I know the Word of God says Jesus forgives all my sins and heals all my diseases, but...." It doesn't matter what you say after the "but," you are negating what you just said.

"I know God's Word says _____" (fill in the blank); however, or although or some other conjunction, and you negate what you just said. Memorize Proverbs 30:5.

The second Scripture to memorize is Matthew 9:35: "Jesus was going through all the cities and villages, teaching in their synagogues and healing every kind of disease and every kind of sickness."

Did Jesus really go about healing *every* kind of disease and sickness? Well, you just said every Word of God is true, and that statement is in the Word of God. Then it is true. Jesus did that back when He walked the earth. But did it end then?

The third verse to memorize: "Jesus Christ is the same yesterday, today, and forever" (Hebrews 13:8). What He did then, He will do now, if we only believe.

That is as complicated as your theology needs to be. All other Scripture will support this basis of belief. I like to say that if God said it, I believe it, I do it, and it *works*.

Chapter 5

How Does Jesus Heal?

There are some with credible healing ministries who maintain that there is a formula to follow—certain specific steps that must be taken—to achieve healing from Jesus. This book is designed to show that, rather than following certain steps, the best thing we can do as individuals and as churches is to provide an environment—an atmosphere—of faith and expectation that allows the Holy Spirit to move as He will to carry out the promises and provisions of the Word of God.

Following are some examples of how people have been healed in our church over the years as we expanded our borders of expectation to allow God to move. We will use fictitious names to protect the privacy of the people involved.

In Worship

The first time I met Fred, I shook his hand and gently patted him on the back. It was like patting the side of a cement wall. The hardness was a cast that resulted from back surgery. Long after the cast was removed, he still had much pain.

One morning in worship, the congregation was singing, and Fred was, too. Suddenly he realized all his pain was gone. No one prayed for him. He was not anointed with oil. He was basking in the manifest presence of God in worship. It had been thirty years since he had gone a day without pain, but he has been pain free all the years since then. In the anointing evident in worship, the Holy Spirit moved upon him and healed him.

Through Prayer

A pregnant woman asked for prayer one Sunday morning. Doctors had discovered a softball-size tumor growing alongside the baby within her.

A member of the congregation laid hands on her and prayed. The woman returned to her doctors and, to their astonishment, they found no tumor. They had not known how to remove the tumor without endangering the baby. God knew.

Sally, who loved to knit and crochet things for her grandchildren, developed osteoarthritis in one wrist and carpal tunnel in the other. She was so disappointed that she couldn't knit gifts anymore, and she asked for prayer. When another woman prayed for her, Sally was healed. Remember that Jesus heals *every* kind of disease and *every* kind of sickness, no matter its name or cause.

Later, Sally shared about her healing with a friend who had a similar problem. The friend's faith was stirred, and she also received healing.

John, a young military man, was concerned that he would be discharged from the Army because of a severe knee injury that resulted in his wearing a knee brace. The knee was basically disintegrated, and doctors saw no hope for recovery. Someone prayed for him, and that same Sunday afternoon he was running around his yard playing ball with his children. The doctors were astounded. He was healed, he no longer needed a brace, and he could stay in the Army.

Through Testimonies

Betty suffered from I.B.S. (Irritable Bowel Syndrome) for twenty-two years. Then she pressed into the Word of God and began to understand and believe Jesus, who not only forgives all our sins, but also heals all our diseases. During a church service, she shared her testimony of being healed! She was so happy to say that she could now eat whatever she wanted.

Shortly afterward, Mary shared that her faith and expectation was so increased by hearing Betty's testimony that she, too, received healing of I.B.S. that she had suffered for eight years.

Sometime later, Cary had expanded her borders of expectation and she, too, was healed after twelve years of the same affliction that the other two women had.

Caleb was born with severe club feet. For two years doctors did all they could, but nothing worked. So an appointment was made with a specialist in a city two hours away.

The boy's grandmother heard of someone who received healing of club feet after *that* person had heard of *another* person's testimony of the same thing. So as Caleb's parents were preparing to take him to the specialist, the grandmother laid hands on him and prayed a fervent prayer that had been stirred by hearing the testimonies.

Upon arrival at the specialist's office two hours later, the parents stood Caleb before the doctor, who asked, "What is he here for?" His feet were perfectly straight! The family has the "before" and "after" photos.

Through the Revelation of God's Love

After hearing the testimony of Caleb's club feet, Sandy went to bed that night overwhelmed by the love God had shown in healing that little boy. That was all that was on her mind as she fell asleep.

As she awoke the next morning, she very carefully and gently got out of bed as usual, because for a long time she had suffered from severe back pain. She hadn't prayed last night about her own need of healing, but as she took a few steps that morning. she realized her back pain was gone!

She evidently expanded her borders of expectation, and that helped her, too, to receive that wonderful manifestation of God's love for herself.

In Response to Intercessory Prayer

A couple in one of the church's home fellowship groups asked if we and their group members would come to pray over their house. They had young twin daughters who suffered from rheumatoid arthritis and were in nearly constant pain, especially at night. They would wake up screaming in pain. The parents had taken the girls to various doctors and had recently returned from the Mayo Clinic with no real solution.

The group went through the house, praying over every room, casting out any demonic spirits, and calling forth God's blessings. The girls were not home at the time. I will always remember laying hands on the girls' beds and praying.

Several days later the mother called and said that the night we all prayed, the girls slept through the night for the first time for a very long time. Their pain was gone. They were healed. Glory to God!

Can you begin to see that the Lord does not need a formula to follow? He just needs an environment of faith and expectation—a people who dare to believe that His Word is true and unchanging.

Because of the Faith of a Child

A mother brought her little girl, Amanda, into the church office one day and told me that Amanda had a very severe allergy to nuts and fruits. If she were to accidentally eat either of them, it could be fatal. She had to carry an Epi Pen with her at all times. She also suffered from asthma.

I asked Amanda if she believed Jesus would heal her. Through a beautiful smile, she said, yes.

After praying, I asked her if she believed she was healed. Through another sweet smile she said, yes.

I felt like the Holy Spirit was telling me that Amanda's faith had made her well. At the same time, I realized that this situation was different from many others. If I were to pray for your injured arm, I might ask you to move it around. If you move it some but then say, ouch, I would pray some more. In this case, the only way to prove she was healed was to give her a bowl of nuts or fruit. I wasn't willing to risk killing her if she didn't really have the faith she claimed.

This was a military family, and they were shortly transferred to another state. We were so thrilled some weeks later to get a lengthy email from the mother. Amanda had been taken for a check-up for school, and they decided to do a thorough exam concerning the allergies and the asthma. The doctor said she had *no asthma* and no sign she ever had it! His conclusion was that it had been a mis-diagnosis. Do I need to tell you that a mother knows if her child has asthma?

As for the life-threatening allergies, she had *no indication of any allergies*. That night she ate a bowl of fruit and was so happy. She had wanted to do that for a long time. Her faith brought her healing. Her parents were very grateful to have learned the importance of the Word of God in their lives, and they have continued to press in and expand the borders of their expectation. Didn't Jesus tell us we should have faith like a child?

Chapter 6

More Ways God Can Heal

Obedience Brings Forth Healing

May I share a personal testimony here? Twenty-five or thirty years ago, as I was mowing the lawn, I became short of breath and had pains in my chest. I went inside to rest.

A neighbor came by to visit with Carolyn, and she began telling about all her relatives who died of heart attacks. I didn't want to hear any more of that, so I excused myself to go take a shower.

As I prepared to shower, I sensed the Holy Spirit telling me to rebuke the spirit of death and break the curse of the generations. In obedience, I rebuked the spirit of death and commanded it to leave. Then I saw a clear vision. The scene was all sand and sky. When I commanded the spirit to leave, it began walking away. It was a hooded figure. Once it turned back toward me and I saw that it had no face. I declared that it must go, so it turned and walked away, becoming smaller until it disappeared into the horizon of sky and sand.

I want to learn as much as I can from such an experience, so I like to replay it over in my mind; but this time I couldn't. The Lord said, "Of course you can't see it. It's gone!" Only many months later was I allowed to recall the vision in order to use it to minister to someone else. After casting that spirit away, I broke the curse of the generations. Several in my family line had experienced heart attacks.

In all the years since, when I get an annual physical exam, the doctors and nurses exclaim what a young heart and wonderful blood pressure I have. Glory be to God!

When performing a miracle, Jesus said: "Did I not say to you that if you believe, you will see the glory of God?" (John 11:40).

Casting out Demons

Sometimes demonic activity is involved in a person's addictions, sickness, or other types of problems, and the demons must be cast out for healing or deliverance to be manifested.

Deliverance may occur within a church service or church activity, or wherever the need occurs. But if you are a part of a church that is open to more of God's involvement in our lives, it doesn't matter so much where it occurs. You are ready for it.

Richard called me late one night and asked if he could come over to our house. Of course I said he could. He was from another nearby community, but he was part of our church. He had an administrative position within the educational system, and he had been struggling with confusion and with not being able to make decisions. As he was telling me all about his issues, the Holy Spirit spoke into my spirit, "Cast out the spirit of the fear of death." So I interrupted Richard and offered to pray for him.

I went over to the couch where he was sitting, laid hands on him, and cast the spirit out. He sunk back into the couch and looked up and said, "How did you know that? I haven't even told my wife that I have been afraid of dying."

Of course I told him I *didn't* know, but the Holy Spirit knows everything about him, and that is why He directed him to come over that night to be delivered.

Christians must be taught about the authority they have in Jesus' name. Many are fearful because of some movie they have seen where a really wild person does all kinds of fear-inducing things because of demons within.

Most of the time demons leave without much fanfare. Once in awhile they will manifest themselves in bizarre ways, but that is not fearful for those who have expanded their borders of faith and expectation to include and understand who they are in Christ.

A pastor friend called one evening and asked if he could bring someone over to our house. The man needed deliverance. Chris was not a part of our church, but I did know him as a leader of a Christian organization. He had several issues. We laid hands on him and began to pray. After a very short time, he lifted his hands and said repeatedly, "Praise the Lord. Praise the Lord."

My first thought was, that was easy! Then the Holy Spirit said, "That is a mocking spirit speaking through him." So I immediately commanded the spirit of mockery to come out of him, and at that moment someone might have been able to make one of those scary movies. He literally bared his teeth, held out his hands like an animal about to claw us, and made various guttural and growling noises.

But there was no fear on our part. We knew the Christ-given authority we had over demons, so five hours later he was free enough to go home and get some rest. We met again the next night and worshiped together, and his deliverance was completed. And I'm pretty sure that the three of us all expanded our borders of expectation after that experience.

> And He went into their synagogues throughout all Galilee, preaching and casting out demons. (Mark 1:39)
>
> And they were casting out many demons and were anointing with oil many sick people and healing them. (Mark 6:13)
>
> And He was casting out a demon, and it was mute; When the demon had gone out, the man spoke; and the crowds were amazed. (Luke 11:14)

One evening, after closing the mid-week church service and getting ready to lock up, we looked back into the sanctuary, and there was a woman kneeling at the altar.

I approached her to see if I might be of some help. She said she had been bothered by demonic spirits, and she thought the problem probably went back to the fact her brother had exposed her to pornography when she was a young teen.

She was shaking and crying. I cast the demons out. She fell over from her kneeling position and lay flat on the floor for several minutes. Then she arose, with her countenance bearing witness to her words: "I am free!" Indeed she was, and she remained free.

Toward the end of another evening church service, several people came forward for prayer. As we laid hands on Bob, he immediately fell backward to the floor. It was his first visit to the church, and I didn't know anything about him.

He hadn't told us why he needed prayer. But the Holy Spirit knew, and He manifested Himself through the gift or manifestation of the discernment of spirits. He showed me to cast out two specific demon spirits, which I did as Bob lay there.

As he came around and began to sit up, I asked him if he was part of a good church. With a big smile on his face that reflected his freedom, he said, "I am now, if you'll have me!"

I'll risk sharing one other of the more dramatic deliverances, but remember that most occasions of casting out demons involve little or no drama. This one occurred before we became pastors. I was still teaching school and also serving as president of the local chapter of the Full Gospel Business Men's Fellowship.

After a Full Gospel meeting was over and people were heading down the stairway, we heard a blood-curdling scream come from upstairs where the meeting had occurred. Carolyn looked at me and said she thought I should go back to see what was going on. Upon re-entering the large room, we saw a young woman who had come to the meeting in a wheel chair. She was now lying on the floor thrashing about and screaming loudly.

The man who had been the evening speaker returned to the room before I did, and he was casting demons out of her. He looked at me and said that there obviously were more, but he wasn't sure what they were.

A guttural voice came from within the woman saying, "I'm going to kill her!" I cast out both the spirit of murder and a spirit of suicide. Her body went limp. She looked up at us with the look of a new-found freedom.

Longer story short—she left pushing the wheel chair in which she had come. The demons had paralyzed her to the point that she had to use the wheel chair. But not any more!

All the glory goes to God, who has given us authority over demons as well as the gifts of the Holy Spirit to aid us in using that authority!

Chapter 7

Expanding the Borders in Your Church

God has placed you in your church for a reason. He wants to use you to help provide an environment of faith and expectation. It takes two things for the expansion to begin and to be successful:

One is leadership that is willing to preach and teach the whole counsel of God, the full Gospel, not just parts of it. If the leadership is resistant, that will hinder the work of the Holy Spirit within your church.

It also takes a congregation that will not only allow the leadership to expand the borders, but will also be supportive of the endeavors.

Pastors have the responsibility to study the Word of God, to pray, and to prepare the messages they bring to the church. They must also be flexible and willing to change their plans if the Holy Spirit begins to lead and move in a different way. A totally formatted and scripted service limits and hinders the spontaneous move of the Holy Spirit.

Congregations must be taught the important difference between just listening to the Word of God as it is preached and really *hearing* what the Holy Spirit is saying to them through that Word. That is when the message becomes revelation in our spirits and not just more knowledge in our minds.

Mark 16:20 says that the Lord confirmed the Word with signs that followed the preaching. Some of the signs are listed in verses seventeen and eighteen.

There are also other ways the Holy Spirit confirms the Word of God today. If the preacher is speaking forth what the Word of God says about healing, faith will be stirred in those who hear the Word, and healing will more likely result if the people are given an opportunity to release their faith and receive it.

If what the Word of God says about forgiveness is spoken under the anointing of the Holy Spirit, some people will be convicted to forgive those they need to forgive—if they are given the opportunity to do so right then. However, if the Word of God is preached regarding forgiveness and then the service ends and the people are dismissed, many will forget and not deal with unforgiveness later.

Matthew 13:18–23 gives some reasons that people may hear the Word but then lose it without acting upon it. For some, the evil one (devil) will steal it from them. Others may hear the Word with joy, but it is only temporary; and when affliction or pressures arise, they fall away from it. Others never respond to the Word because worry or even the deceitfulness of riches may prevent it from bearing fruit in their lives.

The best time for people to respond to the Word in faith is when the anointing is upon it and it is becoming revelation, which will lead to manifestation.

Of course that doesn't mean some people won't respond at a later time. But many will be distracted by other things and lose that moment of faith and conviction that would have released God to manifest His presence and power to confirm the Word.

The same could be said regarding the manifestation, or gifts, of the Holy Spirit that might come forth. If a word of knowledge came forth indicating that someone in the congregation was dealing with a great deal of fear in his life and that a spirit of fear should be cast out, it would not be best to speak that forth and then close the service. It would be best to give that person an opportunity to be prayed for and the spirit of fear cast out then and there.

Not only would that person be set free, but the entire congregation would witness a wondrous work of God and would likely expand the borders of their expectation of what might occur in their church services if they allow the Holy Spirit to move as He desires.

Much of what happens in a church service is directly related to the expectation and faith of the leaders and the congregation. The Apostle Paul said his preaching was not in persuasive words of wisdom, but rather in demonstration of the Holy Spirit and of the power of God. See 1 Corinthians 2:4.

His reason is explained in verse five. He did not want the people to put their faith in the wisdom of men, but in the power of God. Paul could see that, even among churches, there was an increasing ungodliness; and he prophesied that it would get even worse in the last days. He clearly stated that churches were increasingly depending on rituals and traditions of men and were denying the power of God. "....holding to a form of godliness although they have denied its power; avoid such men as these" (2 Timothy 3:5).

God desires to manifest His presence and demonstrate His power among His people as they gather together in faith and expectation. We need to provide an environment that frees Him to do so!

Chapter 8

Even More Ways God Heals

Through Revelation

Revelation brings forth manifestation. The Word becomes alive and active and performs itself in those who believe.

Numerous times we are told in the Bible to *hear* what the Sprit of the Lord is saying. One can listen to the Word of God over and over, but when he really *hears* the Word, it becomes real to him. We must learn to listen with our hearts, not just with our heads.

We were having a series of week-night services, and the last night I preached on what the Word of God says about healing. Afterward we offered an opportunity for those needing a healing of any kind to come forward and someone would pray with them. Remember that Jesus heals all kinds of sickness and disease—physical, mental, emotional, or spiritual. Ann stood up and came forward. She lived in another town but had been invited to the service by a friend. Another woman prayed with her.

Sometime later, Ann came back to share her testimony. She had suffered with very painful degenerative discs in her back. For thirty years she had gone through five major back surgeries and had been on many different kinds of medications but had found no relief from any of it. She didn't just listen to the preaching that night, but she *heard* the word in her spirit. It became revelation, and the revelation became manifestation. She was healed completely. She went back to her doctor, who was astounded; and after thorough examination, he took her off all medications.

When Ann was healed, I am sure she expanded her borders of faith and expectation because of the wonderful healing she received after so many years of suffering. She now believed the Word of God.

Through Revelation from Scripture

One Sunday afternoon Kathy called. She said that, before she was saved, she had an abortion. Since then every time she heard someone talking about abortion, tremendous grief would nearly overwhelm her. She had not told anyone about it, but she could hardly stand to bear the grief anymore. I shared some Scriptures with her, especially Isaiah 53:4: "Surely our griefs He Himself bore, and our sorrows He carried." Jesus took that upon Himself when He went to cross on her behalf.

After the call was over, Carolyn asked who it was and what was going on. I told her and then said that I did not feel like I was of much help to her. I just quoted some Scriptures and tried to encourage her to accept and receive what Jesus had done for her.

Kathy later told me she had felt the same way after she hung up the phone. Pastor just quoted some Scriptures that she already knew. But she said for some reason she took her Bible and looked up Isaiah 53 once again, and when she read verse four, she said it was like a spotlight was shined on it and it lept off the page and into her heart. A day or two later a young man came up to her and asked a question about abortion. After the conversation, she realized the grief, the sorrow, and the pain were gone.

When the Word becomes revelation, it then becomes manifestation. "...the word of God which performs its work in you who believe" (1 Thessalonians 2:13b). Part of expanding the borders of our faith and expectation is learning to allow the Holy Spirit to bring revelation from God's written Word so it can become real and working in our lives, both in our individual lives and in our churches.

Diane had a breakdown and went berserk. She ended up in a mental hospital in a padded cell. She would not speak with any of her family. Her brother was just learning about healing, faith, and the Word of God, but he did not know what to do. So he sent her a very brief letter with three or four Scriptures in it.

Long story short—she read them and was healed and released from the institution. There is power in the word of God! "He sent His word and healed them and delivered them from their destructions" (Psalm 107:20).

Healing Through Forgiveness

A man in our church had an angioplasty procedure in which they run a tube up through the groin into the heart. In the process, an error was made, and the main nerve to his leg was severed. That kind of nerve can not grow back. Consequently, he could only drag that leg along if he had things to hold onto. He could not walk; and for three years he was restricted to bed or a wheelchair.

During that time he became increasingly bitter toward the doctors, and his bitterness began to affect his marriage. He quit coming to church because he became bitter toward God, too.

After an extended absence from church, he appeared one Sunday morning. It was the end of the service, and the people were standing. I had just said amen to the closing prayer when his daughter helped him struggle forward.

I asked what he wanted, and his reply indicated that he believed God would heal him, and he asked if we would pray for him. Because we had developed an environment of expectation, the people remained in place.

I laid hands on him and began to pray, and after a few seconds he declared, "It's hot, It's hot," placing his hand on the afflicted leg. He began to sink to the floor, and he was given a chair to sit on.

I called the entire congregation to come forward and surround him and join together in prayer. The service had concluded, but it was not over. The people came and prayed a few more minutes.

Then he abruptly stood up and requested that no one touch him. He told us all that the doctors had told him he would never walk again and certainly would never be able to climb stairs.

Looking at the stairs that lead to the platform, he quickly went up the stairs, then back down, back up, and again back down! The church celebrated! Then he walked out of the church normally, and he has been walking ever since.

Later he shared his testimony of how he came to the point that he was willing to forgive the doctors, even as Christ had forgiven him of all the mistakes he had made in life. After he had forgiven them and others who the Lord brought to remembrance, he knew the Lord would heal him that day if he would return to church and humble himself and ask for prayer.

He requested an appointment with the doctor to re-test the nerve. It was a painful test in which long needles were inserted several places in the leg to check the functionality of the nerve. Five meant it was perfectly normal; zero meant it had no function at all. The test result was a five! The medical staff were in tears as they declared that there is no way that nerve could have grown back together and allowed him to walk after three years.

With God, all things are possible!

Many things can hinder our receiving the promises and provisions of God. Unforgiveness is a major one. Expanding our borders of expectation certainly includes the significance of forgiveness.

Helping Even Your Own Family Members

Have you ever heard the statement that you can't help your own family members? You may be able to help others, but members of your own family will not receive your help. I hope after reading the following testimony you will reject that statement and realize that, when we follow the leading of the Holy Spirit in our lives and continue to expand our borders of expectation, He can and will do wonders.

About twenty-five years ago the Holy Spirit instructed me to go minister to my mother about forgiveness. She lived about two and a half hours away from us. I called her and asked if I could come visit her the following Saturday. She indicated that I would be welcome.

I went, sat across the room from her in her living room, and reminded her that she had suffered many afflictions, had numerous surgeries, and had even been written up in medical journals regarding things that were very real but that the medical people could not figure out. I reminded her that she had been hurt many times, even by her own children, and that the answer to all these afflictions was forgiveness of those who had hurt her.

I explained from the Scriptures that we are instructed to forgive others as Jesus forgave us (Ephesians 4:31–32).

He did not feel like going to the cross, He wasn't saying we were right, but He forgave us while we were still in sin. If we forgive as He forgave us, we don't have to *feel* like forgiving those who have hurt us, we are not saying they are right, and they may still be wrong.

He forgave us in obedience to Father God, and that is the same reason we are to forgive. In His Word, He has instructed us to do so.

All the time I was sharing with her she was drinking a large glass of ice tea, and she was crying much of the time. After forty-five minutes I was thinking, "Lord, she isn't even getting what I'm trying to tell her. I'm taking five or six hours out of my Saturday and she isn't even getting it."

Finally, I said, "Mom, that is all I came to tell you." She excused herself to go to the bathroom. That is where the large glass of tea comes into the story.

Dad and I waited quietly for what seemed like a very long time. She was still in the bathroom. A thought came into my mind: "She is in there taking some of the several medications she is on. You brought her under condemnation, and you had better get in there right now."

At the same time, the Holy Spirit spoke into my spirit the Bible verse that says we should take every thought into captivity unto the obedience of Christ (2 Corinthians 10:5). I knew the first thought was not from God, so we continued to wait a little longer.

We must have let out a sigh of relief when we heard the bathroom door open. This disheveled-looking woman who had entered the bathroom came out with a glow on her face, hugged me, and said, "Thank you, Son, for coming to share with me today."

I did not have to ask. I knew then that she did get it. She did receive it. She had been in that bathroom forgiving those who had hurt her. I was so glad I didn't knock and interrupt her.

And, glory to God, I must tell you that she was not sick again for the rest of her fifteen or so years of life except that she got the 24-hour flu that swept through their apartment complex once or twice. Forgiveness brings healing.

Healing in Response to a Word of Knowledge

A word of knowledge is one of the gifts of the Holy Spirit (1 Corinthians 12:1–11). It occurs when He gives you information or knowledge about a person or situation that you have no other way of knowing.

Even as we pursue love, we are to earnestly desire spiritual gifts. See 1 Corinthians 14:1. We are to desire and seek after the manifestations of the Holy Spirit, because they are extremely helpful in ministering to people's real needs.

One example: A young lady poured out her heart, listing numerous problems she had. I thought, where do we even begin to help her? The Holy Spirit spoke into my spirit saying that all her troubles stem from her having been sexually molested when she was fourteen years old.

So I asked her the question: "Did anything significant happen in your life when you were fourteen years old?" Immediately it was as if a dam broke as her tears poured forth like a flood. She shared that, when she was fourteen years old, she was sexually assaulted by several relatives. *Now* we had the root of all her problems and we could focus on that.

I often compare people's problems with dandelions. You can attempt to pull a dandelion out of the ground, you may spray it with a herbicide or try other ways to get rid of it, but unless you remove it by the roots, it will keep coming back.

The manifestations—or gifts—of the Holy Spirit often help you get to the root of someone's problems and save a great deal of counseling, time, energy, and dead ends. And they make your ministry more efficient and effective.

As you expand the borders of your faith and expectation, learn about the gifts of the Spirit and their value.

During a church service, a word of knowledge came forth indicating that there was someone who had an injured left shoulder that God wanted to heal. I knew nothing about Ian's injury, but God did.

He came forward, and as he was walking to the platform area, he was healed. I told him to move his arm around. He did so freely in all directions, and he was overcome and amazed at the healing!

On another occasion, a special speaker emphasized the importance of forgiveness. He spoke of the freedom that comes when we release all unforgiveness.

A man in the audience was listening intently, and afterward I saw him sitting alone with tears in his eyes. I went to him to see if I could be of help. He said he grew up with a poor relationship with his father, but he had forgiven him of the things he had done to him, yet he still had not found freedom.

The Holy Spirit gave me a word of knowledge. I said, "You have forgiven your father for all the things he did to you. Have you forgiven him for all the things he did *not* do? For the times he never came to your ball games to see you play, the times he never told you he was proud of you when you accomplished something worthwhile, the times he passed by you and never patted your back or tousled your hair?"

At that point the tears were no longer just in his eyes, but rolling down his entire face and pouring to the ground! We prayed together, and he forgave his father for things he had not done. And the man found the freedom of true forgiveness!

Other Ways Healing May Come in an Environment of Expectation

During a communion service, the message was on believing God's word and receiving His promises. The people were challenged to reach out with their faith and receive any healing they needed.

The next Sunday a pre-teen boy shared that he had scoliosis (curvature of the spine), and as he partook of the elements of communion, he received his healing. He was thrilled to be able to show us all how he could bend over and touch the floor, something he was not able to do before.

Can you begin to see that we do not need to follow a specific formula to experience the wonders of God in our midst? We just need to develop an atmosphere of expectation and keep on expanding our borders, allowing the Holy Spirit to move freely among us.

Chapter 9

Is It Real?

Probably if you are a real skeptic, you have not read this far. But you may be among those who have some doubts, because you have seen someone on television, or even in a church, abuse or misuse the gifts of the Spirit. Maybe you concluded that it is all counterfeit, so you will avoid expanding your borders of expectation beyond what you already have experienced and with which you are comfortable.

Two thoughts to consider: Are you avoiding learning more and experiencing more of the manifestations of the Holy Spirit because some whackos and charlatans are out there? If you are avoiding the gifts of the Spirit, are you also avoiding the fruit of the Spirit—love, joy, peace, etc.? (Galatians 5:22).

You surely know that there are many who abuse, misuse, or even counterfeit the *fruit* of the Spirit by substituting promiscuous sex for love, alcohol for joy, drugs for peace, etc. Yet you probably desire and long for more of His love, joy, peace, and the rest of the fruit. If it is in the Word of God, it is real. Both the fruit and the gifts are real.

Why Are Some Not Healed?

We do not need to avoid asking this question. In fact we should ask it and pursue its answer.

One of the greatest barriers that prevent many people from expanding their borders in the area of healing is that they know someone who is a very nice Christian person who has not been able to receiving healing from God.

Below is a partial list of biblical reasons our prayers may be hindered or our faith may seem to be ineffective in any area.

Some Hindrances to Receiving Healing
(Not a complete list)

1. Unforgiveness (Ephesians 4:31–2)
2. Worry (Philippians 4:6) and fear (Matthew 8:23–27)
3. Doubt (James 1:5–8)
4. Unbelief (John 4:48)
5. Discouragement (Nehemiah 4:10)
6. Entanglement of sin (Hebrews 12:1–2)
7. Lack of knowledge or understanding of God's Word (Hosea 4:6)
8. Ungrateful heart (Psalm 26:1–7, & 69:29-30, Colossians 2:6–7)
9. Situations that look impossible (Luke 5:18–26, Mark 5:25–34)
10. Unbelieving friends & relatives (Mark 5:35–42)

11. Scoffers & mockers (John 9:1–38)
12. Lack of concern for the hurting (Matthew 15:23)
13. Love of worldly possessions (Matthew 19:21–22)
14. Potential loss of disability payments if healed, & other forms of deceitfulness of riches (Mark 4:19)
15. Opposition to the truth (2 Timothy 3:7–9)
16. Neglecting to keep faith strong by praying in the Spirit (Jude 20, 1 Corinthians 14:4)
17. Priorities out of order (Philippians 3:7–8)
18. Disobedience to the word of God (James 1:22)
19. No corresponding action with what person says he believes (James 2:17, 20, 26)
20. Dishonoring spouse (1 Peter 3:7)
21. Lack of endurance (Hebrews 10:23, 35–36).
22. Falling away from faith because of persecution or affliction (Mark 4:17)
23. Desire for worldly things (Mark 4:19)
24. Strong ties to unbelieving family or church (Matthew 10:37–38)
25. Occult involvement (Deuteronomy 18:9–12, Isaiah 8:19)

It may well be that you know some people who have not received a healing, and as far as you can tell, none of the above seem to apply to them.

This is not meant to be a complete list; and in addition, I will share with you a comment I heard many years ago from a preacher addressing this issue. He said, "Always remember that the Holy Spirit knows at least one more thing than you do about a person or a situation."

We should realize that none of us has all the answers to every situation. Unless the Holy Spirit reveals a specific reason someone has been hindered in receiving from God, be sure to remember that it is not your job to judge him or in any way condemn him. If you do, it will probably be only a matter of time until the Lord will allow something to come upon you to see how *you* handle a similar situation.

> Trust in the Lord with all your heart and do not lean on your own understanding. In all your ways acknowledge Him and He will make your path straight. (Proverbs 3:5–8)

While pondering in your mind why someone seems not to be receiving a provision of God, realize that the question goes beyond the area of healing. Have you not known good Christian people who just never have received the wonderful gift of peace that Jesus offers us? They seem to worry and be fearful.

Have you ever known a nice Christian who seems never to have gotten hold of the comfort that the Lord has so clearly offered his followers?

I am not talking about self-centeredness here; but our priority should be expanding the borders of our own faith and expectation. As we do, we will find the Holy Spirit becoming more active in our life and more available to give us whatever insight we really need in a situation.

One might look at the list above and think he must have to be perfect in every area of life to receive anything from God. No. You were saved while you were in sin. But you repented when you learned about Jesus and that He would forgive your sins. However, after you learned about Jesus, if you had refused to repent of your known sin and turn to Him, you would not have received the salvation that He had for you.

In a similar manner, if you learn from the Word of God that He calls you to forgive, to treat your spouse with honor, or any of the other hindrances listed previously, and you refuse to do those things, they remain an open door to various kinds of sickness and disease.

We must choose either to obey and follow His Word and His ways or to reject Him and His ways. We must choose to close the doors that allow sickness and disease to come in.

What If They Do Not Respond?

What if you share something the Holy Spirit seems to be showing you about the root or cause of someone's problem or situation, and the person does not respond? Fair question.

Don came to our church for the first time, and a word of knowledge came forth that someone in attendance was suffering from very severe migraine headaches, and the Lord wanted to heal the person. An invitation was given to come forward for prayer. No one responded.

Don later told the church member who had brought him to that service that the word was for him. He had suffered from severe migraines for a long time. But he said he would soon get out of the military and would get pretty nice disability payments. If he received healing, he would not get the payments. So he bypassed an opportunity for the Lord to heal him because of the deceitfulness of riches.

Another time a word of knowledge came forth that the Lord desired to heal someone of club feet and another person of a heart condition. No one responded.

A few days later a young man came to me in tears and shared that he had felt the Holy Spirit telling him he was to bring his parents to church that Sunday. He did not obey. One of his parents had club feet; the other had a bad heart. I think the young man learned something of the importance of obedience.

We can not be responsible for how people respond to things that we share in love, but we can provide an atmosphere of faith and expectation so increasing numbers *will* respond as they experience the wonders of God and as they hear testimonies of others who are expanding their borders.

Chapter 10

Why Be Concerned About Healing and Deliverance?

Because Jesus always has been! "The Son of God appeared for this purpose, to destroy the works of the devil" (1 John 3:8). Sin and sickness are the works of darkness—Satan's domain.

> You know of Jesus of Nazareth, how God anointed Him with the Holy Spirit and with power, and how He went about doing good and healing all who were oppressed by the devil, for God was with Him. (Acts 10:38)

After spending about three years walking the earth proclaiming the Kingdom of God, healing the sick, and casting out demons, Jesus began to send His followers out to do the same things.

> Truly, truly, I say to you, he who believes in Me, the works that I do, he will do also; and greater works than these he will do because I go to the Father. (John 14:12)

> Jesus summoned His twelve disciples and gave them authority over unclean spirits, to cast them out, and to heal every kind of disease and every kind of sickness. (Matthew 10:1)

Jesus was delegating His authority to His disciples. He was sending them out to exercise that authority.

Then we read in the tenth chapter of Luke that He sent seventy others out with the same instructions. In verse nine, He specifically told them to heal the sick and proclaim the Kingdom of God. They went forth and did as He had instructed. Upon their return, they were rejoicing over the authority they had, even over demons.

As we expand our boundaries of faith and expectation, we must learn and accept the authority Jesus has given His followers over demons. Demons have power, but we not only have power, but in addition, we have authority.

Authority supercedes power. Think of an eighteen-wheel truck loaded with steel coming down the highway at the speed limit. If a 160-pound man stepped out in front of the truck, he would be crushed and destroyed. However, if that man was in a law enforcement uniform and recognized as a police officer, he could stop that truck by simply holding up his hand. The truck driver knows he has the power to crush the officer but that, if he did, he would have the entire judicial system after him. He is not facing just a man, but a whole system.

Likewise, when a Spirit-filled Christian is wearing the "full armor of God" as described in Ephesians 6:10–17, demons know they face not just that person who has been deputized by Jesus, but they face the entire judicial system of Heaven!

"In Jesus' name" means in His authority. It is like a law enforcement officer saying to a felon behind a closed door, "Open up in the name of the law!"

Just before Jesus ascended back into Heaven, He gave His followers some instructions. Read Matthew 28:18–20 and Mark 16:15–20. Here He is commissioning them to go into all the world in His authority and do the works that He had done: proclaim the Kingdom, heal the sick, and cast out demons.

He commanded them to "observe" all that He had told them and to teach others to do likewise. The word observe here is not as it is used to view something or to see something. Here it means *do*. It is like observing the speed limit. You don't drive any speed you want as long as you *look* at the speed limit signs as you drive by them. It means you *do* what they say to do.

Elsewhere Jesus said that He was sending His followers out in the same way the Father had sent Him: To destroy the works of the devil, to proclaim the Kingdom, and to heal the sick. That is how He was sent.

Chapter 11

Changing Jurisdictions

As you continue to expand your borders, you will at some point realize that, as a Christ-follower, you have changed jurisdictions. This is a very important concept that many Christians have not yet gotten hold of, and it is a life-changer for both individuals and churches.

As you read through the second and third chapters of Ephesians, you see that, although we formerly walked in darkness according to the prince of the power of the air, when we were born again, God raised us up with Him and seated us with Him in the heavenly places in Christ Jesus. Obviously, we are not physically seated in that position, but we have been positionally seated together with Christ, sharing in the authority He has given us over the spirits and forces of darkness.

Let us note here that, as believers, we have changed jurisdictions. We now serve a new master; yet the old one still tries to deceive us into serving him.

When I was in the Army and my sergeant hollered, I jumped into obedience. He had rightful authority over me. I knew it, and he knew it.

But when I got out of the Army, I changed jurisdictions. I changed the authority system. The only way he could exercise authority over me now would be if I would submit to him, even though he no longer has any legal authority over me.

When you were born, you were born into a sinful world filled with spiritual darkness. When you were born again, you were transferred into a new realm. You have a new master, and the former one has no rightful legal authority over you any more! The only way the demon spirits of darkness can rule over you now is if you let them. They have no right to do so.

As you continue to expand your borders and press into learning more of what the Word of God says, you will find yourself walking stronger in your rightful, legal, Christ-given, Holy Spirit empowered authority over the powers of darkness. "Behold, I have given you authority to tread upon serpents and scorpions, and over all the power of the enemy...." (Luke 10:19).

As we expand our borders of faith and expectation, we should move more and more in Jesus' authority and in the power of His Spirit. Remember that "the greater One is in you" if you are a born-again believer and follower of Jesus. See 1 John 4:4.

Chapter 12

How Does Faith Fit In?

"Faith is the assurance of things hoped for, the conviction of things not yet seen" (Hebrews 11:1).

"Without faith it is impossible to please God, for he who comes to God must believe that He is and that He is a rewarder of those who seek Him" (Hebrews 11:6).

Faith carries with it a strong expectation, a knowing. It is being fully persuaded. It is the bridge between our needs and God's provision.

Faith has learned God's promises, believes them, declares them, and acts upon them.

Faith brings the promises into manifestation. Bible faith works.

Sometimes hope is confused with faith. Even fear may look similar to faith. Someone says, "I'm having surgery next week. I really don't want to have surgery. I am standing in faith that Jesus will heal me so I won't need it." How many things do you see wrong with such a statement?

This does not reflect unwavering faith. Faith is the assurance of things not yet seen. It is knowing that what you are declaring will come to pass. There is no need for alternate plans.

> But he must ask in faith without any doubting, for the one who doubts is like the surf of the sea, driven and tossed by the wind. For that man ought not to expect that he will receive anything from the Lord, being a double-minded man, unstable in all his ways. (James 1:6–8)

Chapter 13

What Does Our Salvation Include?

What did Jesus purchase for us when He shed His blood on the cross. We say He saved us; He purchased our salvation. Some say He made it possible for those who believe in and follow Him to have eternal life in Heaven. That is true, but there is more.

Some say He shed His blood to forgive our sins. That is also true, but there is more. He exchanged our sins for His righteousness (2 Corinthians 5:21).

Let's look even further at the word "save" or "salvation" to see what the original Hebrew and Greek languages of the Bible have to say.

Yeshuwah, Teshuawa, and Tesha in the Hebrew and Soteria and Sodezo in the Greek all include the following as part of their definition and usage: deliverance, aid, victory, health, help, save, welfare, rescue, freedom, and make whole. Those are not things you will need in heaven. Those are things you need in this life on earth.

As we expand our borders of faith and expectation, we see that Jesus provided a great deal that we can continue to appropriate as we learn how.

It Is All Part of the Script

A script for a play or speech is a written plan that is to be followed. We call God's script or His written plan the Scripture.

Jesus spoke of the script when He said, "...that all things which are written about Me in the Law of Moses and the Prophets and the Psalms must be fulfilled" (Luke 24:44).

One example of what the Psalms said is as follows: "Bless the Lord, O my soul, and forget none of His benefits. He pardons all your iniquities. He heals all your diseases" (Psalm 103:2–3).

One of the prophets said about Jesus, who was yet to come:

> Surely our griefs He Himself bore, and our sorrows He carried; yet we ourselves esteemed Him stricken, smitten of God, and afflicted. He was pierced through for our transgressions. He was crushed for our iniquities. The chastening for our well-being fell upon Him, and by His scourging (stripes) we are healed. (Isaiah 53:4–5)

Jesus said all things written about Him *must* be fulfilled. Why? Because they were a part of God's script. Healing and deliverance are surely a part of our salvation.

Chapter 14

Is There Anything Better Than Healing?

There is something better than healing. That is not getting sick. Walking in health is much more conducive to our ability to minister to others.

Hospitals and other institutions for the sick are crowded. Medical costs are soaring. Sickness and disease seem to be all around us. Even so, it is not often mentioned that most sickness is preventable.

Preventable? Yes, many diseases are caused by smoking, alcohol, and sexual promiscuity. The one who does not smoke or drink and is faithful in marriage prevents many types of diseases.

Overeating, poor diet, and lack of exercise can also cause a variety of physical problems. Again, we can control these things and eliminate their associated afflictions.

Another major cause of disease is our reaction to stress and the pressures of life. This, too, can be prevented. Stress can affect every system of our bodies.

There is not room here for a thorough discussion, but below are some common afflictions known to be caused by our reaction to stress and pressures of life.

- Digestive disorders
- Eliminative disorders
- Difficulty in swallowing
- Asthma and other respiratory diseases
- High blood pressure and diseases of blood vessels
- Heart diseases, strokes, coronary thrombosis
- Coagulation dysfunction
- Skin diseases of various kinds
- Arteriosclerosis
- Arthritis
- Migraine headaches
- Excessive fatigue
- Eye problems
- Mononucleosis
- Hyperthyroidism
- Menstrual and menopausal disorders
- Obesity
- Certain tumors and cancers
- Infertility and impotence
- Kidney disorders
- Retarded physical growth
- Premature aging

I have written a booklet, "Victory over Stress and Disease," that goes into more detail.

For now, be encouraged by these Scriptures:

> Peace I leave with you. My peace I give unto you. I do not give to you as the world gives. Do not let your heart be troubled, and do not be afraid. (John 14:27)

> Be anxious for nothing, but in everything by prayer and supplication with thanksgiving let your requests be made known to God. And the peace of God, which surpasses all comprehension, shall guard your hearts and your minds in Christ Jesus. (Philippians 4:6–7)

> Now may the God of hope fill you with all joy and peace in believing, that you may abound in hope by the power of the Holy Spirit. (Romans 15:13)

Expand your borders of faith and expectation. Learn more about and experience the tremendous peace the Lord has for you in all situations. It will be well worth the effort. A Christian need not allow his heart to be fearful or in turmoil. "For God has not given us a spirit of fear, but of power and love and discipline" (2 Timothy 1:7).

"For He Himself is our peace... " (Ephesians 2:14).

Hindrances to Our Expansion

As you determine to expand your borders of faith and expectation, you are likely to encounter some resistance.

Denominational teaching, unbelieving friends and relatives, even demonic resistance—these and many other things can rob you of your determination and desire to learn and experience more of the wonders of God. Jesus said, "The thief comes only to steal and kill and destroy. I came that they may have life, and have it abundantly" (John 10:10).

Chapter 15

Is It All About Healing and Deliverance?

In this book we have used testimonies of healing as examples of some of the wondrous things God will do, all in accordance with His Word. Let us look at a few other areas.

God provides all we need for life. "His divine power has granted to us everything pertaining to life and godliness, through the true knowledge of Him who called us by His own glory and excellence" (2 Peter 1:3).

Material Needs

"He delights in the prosperity of His servant" (Psalm 35:27).

Whoa! Don't put the book down yet. No, we are not speaking here that God owes us a jet plane, a million dollar home, and three luxury cars. That kind of thinking is not biblical.

Biblical prosperity refers to our well being. Our needs are met. Surely we do not need to take up space here explaining the difference between our needs, wants, and desires, so we won't.

I well remember the time many years ago when a friend came to me and handed me an envelope. He said, "God told me to give this to you." Inside was a fifty dollar bill. That caused me to realize I needed to expand the borders of any faith and expectation I had at the time. I was not only overwhelmed by the money gift, but also by the fact that God would tell someone to help provide for some needs I had but that the man knew nothing about.

Speaking of needs, when our boys were small, one needed some extensive dental work. We met with the dentist for a consultation, and he explained the procedure and said it would cost three hundred dollars. My reply was "Do you mean for each appointment?" He said no, that would be the total cost.

A few years later our other son needed similar dental work, so we set up another consultation with the dentist, and on the way I prayed, "Oh, Lord, let it be a relatively small bill like it was with our other son." After explaining the procedure, the dentist said it would cost $1,720. Keep in mind that this was probably thirty-five years ago, and that was a *lot* of money back then.

This did not seem to be an answer to my sincere prayer for a low bill. I had no idea how we would manage such an amount, yet I had a peace in my heart about it and said, okay.

Have I mentioned that God does not like to be put in a box? Not long after, we got a knock on our door. It was a man we knew. He handed me an envelope and said that he and his wife had sold some land and wanted to give a tithe off of it to Carolyn and me as gratitude for helping them work through some issues in their marriage.

Note: This all took place before we were called into the pastorate. We would not have taken payment for helping someone in our capacity as pastors.

Anyway, he turned and left, and I looked in the envelope. Now this man knew nothing about the recent dental bill of $1,720. Inside the envelope was a check for $1,722. I still have not figured out what the extra two dollars were for.

Can you imagine that the borders of my faith and expectation were expanded through this experience? Even in more ways than one, as you will see.

I called the man and told him that I was not even sure I could accept such a kind offer, but that I would pray about it and get back to him. While praying about it, the Lord clearly reminded me what the Word of God says: "It is more blessed to give than to receive" (Acts 20:35). He then said, "How can I bless the one who gave to you unless you receive it?" That was a new concept for me. It had been beyond my borders.

So I let the man know that I received his generous gift with much gratitude and that I knew God would bless him for it. Shortly after, both he and his wife were healed of physical conditions that they had suffered for some time. Sounds like sowing and reaping, does it not?

So does that mean God is going to provide for all our needs by having other people give us money? Of course not. We have worked hard all our lives for our income and will continue to do so. But there are times when God may choose to use others, and when He does, it involves our learning much from it and expanding our borders. We must learn not only to be good givers, but also we must learn how to be good receivers!

Sometimes God Provides for Something Better Than What We Ask For

Have you noticed that sometimes God responds to our prayers in a way different than we thought He would?

Before we were in full-time ministry, there was a time when our washing machine broke down, our car needed repairs, and there was one other major need that I don't recall now what it was. I was praying that God would help us meet those needs.

The next day someone at the high school where I was teaching congratulated me on winning the new suit. He said he heard on the radio that morning that a new men's clothing store had offered a suit to the winner of a drawing. I had not entered a drawing. I didn't even know a new store was opening.

I immediately thought of Carolyn and called her. She said she had seen the ad for the drawing and, somehow, just felt she was to drive to the store and enter. This was not something she would ordinarily do.

My response was, "Lord, my washing machine is broken, my car needs repairs, and this other thing needs to be fixed. I don't need a suit. I already have one."

As soon as I was quiet, I heard on the inside of me, "I am going to put you in places where you can wear the suit, tell how you got it, and glorify Me."

Shortly afterward I began to get invitations from Full Gospel Business Men's Fellowship groups around the state to come share my testimony and minister to the people in attendance. Guess what I wore to each of those meetings!

Oh, by the way, the washing machine began to work fine, the car repairs turned out to be very minor, and whatever that other thing was, it was okay, too.

The lessons I learned through all this were far more valuable and have lasted far longer than the suit. One of the big ones was that God will supply not only the needs of which I am aware, but will even provide for needs of which I don't yet know.

The following Scripture took on a new meaning: "Therefore let us draw near with confidence to the throne of grace, so that we may receive mercy and find grace in time of need" (Hebrews 4:16).

When I went to the clothing store, I did not peek in the alley window and ask if I could talk to someone about the offer of a free suit. I walked in the front door boldly, gave the employee my name, and told him I was there to claim my suit.

What gave me such boldness? The store had made a public contract with its ad declaring that they would give a suit to the winner of the drawing. Why can we go with boldness and confidence to God to claim what has become ours? We can because He made a public contract with provisions for those who qualify!

Better than a contract, we have a covenant with Him! I pray these testimonies bring glory to God and that they help and encourage you to take the limitations off of Him.

He Will Supply the Needs of Individuals and Churches That Endeavor to Follow Him.

The church we pastored was looking for larger facilities. We ended up purchasing a sixty-five-thousand square foot building and twenty-one acres of land for one hundred thousand dollars. It was a run-down industrial building into which members of the church built beautiful facilities. Do you think that may have taken some faith and expectation? It would take another book to tell that story.

If your church has come together in love and unity and is sincerely doing what it can to expand its borders of faith and expectation, you can look forward to the Lord's help and provision as needs arise. Do what you can, and He will make up the difference!

Let me say it again. God does not just pour out blessings like this every day. I'm sharing some highlights in this book for a few reasons. One is to glorify God. Another is to encourage you not to put limits on Him; do not put Him in a box.

Yet another reason is that, worked in around all the testimonies included in this book, I'm offering you some principles that might encourage you to press in and expand your borders of faith and expectation. I told the Lord when I accepted the call to ministry that I would never try to teach others something I have not learned and experienced myself. For example, I will not teach others about the importance of forgiveness if I have not rid unforgiveness from my own life.

Let Him Use You to Help Others

As you continue to learn from the Word of God that the Holy Spirit desires to work in and through you, and in and through your church, He will be able to use you even more.

A pastor from another town stopped by one day. We had never met, but he just needed someone to talk to. He was highly discouraged, and it sounded like he was having big problems in his church and could even lose his ministry.

I didn't know anything about him in the natural. I didn't know whether he was married or not; but I sensed the Holy Spirit was prompting me to ask him to rate his marriage on a scale of one to ten, one being the worst it could be, ten the best.

His reply indicated it would be about two on that scale. Again by the prompting of the Lord, I told him that was the root of all his problems in the church, and if he would get before God and begin to apply the Word of God to his marriage, that would take care of both the marriage and the church problems.

Chapter 16

Are Some Miracles
Hard to Believe?

Let's say some are more so than others. Sometimes it is not so much that they are hard to believe, but that we just feel more confident sharing them with others when they have been validated somehow. Maybe it should not be that way. Maybe we need to expand the borders in that area.

For example, we had a woman from out of town visit a Sunday morning church service. Evidently someone prayed for her. Several days later I got a letter from the woman saying she was en route to a nearby city to have brain surgery that week, but she went through our town on Sunday and decided to stop in for a church service.

The next day she went to her destination, and she said that, after multiple tests, the doctors could not find the cancer for which they had scheduled the surgery!

The woman did not leave an address or way of contacting her, and we never heard from her again. With all the healings we have observed, it is not really difficult to believe her story. It just would have been nice to have had some documentation from the doctors or an opportunity to follow up with her for the sake of sharing her story with skeptics.

In another situation, a man I knew well told us that his daughter had gone to the grocery one evening, and upon returning to the parking lot to get into her car, she noticed a group of men staring at her. As she started the car and drove past them, their mouths dropped open and their eyes bulged. She wondered what was going on.

When she got home and told her dad, he said it sounded like they had planned to do her harm, but something intervened. He looked at her car and found that the battery was missing. The men had apparently taken the battery out of the car while she was in the store, and knowing she would not have been able to start it, they would have moved in with evil intentions.

Do I need to mention that cars do not normally start without a battery? This was a miracle that superseded the natural laws of mechanics. When I heard this story, my boundaries of faith and expectation were expanded. I could believe the story because I knew the man who told it, and he was a man of impeccable integrity.

Speaking of car batteries, there was a time I came out of a store and saw two young military men with the hood of their car raised. They asked me if I had a jumper cable they could borrow to start their car. I did not have one at the time, but I experienced something akin to, on a lesser level, a "silver and gold have I none, but such as I have give I thee" moment.

They told me they had to get back to their duty station shortly, and if they didn't, they would be in big trouble. I went over and looked and remembered that I had been learning that there is power and authority in Jesus' name. I told them to get in the car. They did. I then laid hands on the battery and commanded quietly, but with authority, "Battery, in Jesus' name, work!" I told the soldier in the driver's seat, "Try it now." He turned the key, the battery sounded, and the engine started.

With eyes opened very wide, the man asked, "What did you do?" My reply was, "I don't know what you guys know about the power of Jesus' name, but I laid hands on your battery and commanded it to start, and it did." Their eyes had not yet returned to normal size when I told them that I would love to tell them more about it, but they had better get going so they would not be in trouble for being late. They agreed and sped off while waving and shouting many thanks.

Okay, so does this mean that any time our vehicle battery goes dead, we can resurrect it by the same method I used? No. I am convinced that God wanted to help these two young men in such a way that they would remember this event and He might send others into their lives to witness the Gospel to them.

Someone reading that account may be thinking the whole thing was just a coincidence. Sometimes a battery will start after sitting awhile. Well, it hadn't had a chance to rest. They were constantly trying to get it to turn over.

How you view such a testimony probably depends on how far you have expanded your borders of expectation. If I had a jumper cable, I would have used that to help them; but there are times when we do not have a natural means to solve a problem, and we must learn to expect that God is there to help us do what we can not do ourselves.

Remember the words from the Bible that say nothing is impossible with God. Remembering these words of truth will help you and your church expand your borders of faith and expectation.

Chapter 17

Getting Rid of the Rats

> Therefore since we have so great a cloud of witnesses surrounding us, let us also lay aside every encumbrance and the sin which so easily entangles us, and let us run with endurance the race that is set before us. (Hebrews 12:1)

How many times is the word "us" used in the Scripture above? That means us and our churches.

God has a plan for your life and for your church, and we are to run that race with endurance and lay hold of all He has for us in order to succeed in that calling.

It seems that "staying power" is often lacking in Christian lives. It is so easy to just give in or give up before obtaining what God has for us. We find it difficult to "lay aside every encumbrance and sin" as spoken of above.

Earlier we spoke of the importance of getting to the root of a problem, using the analogy of a dandelion. Perhaps another analogy here will be helpful.

If you want to get rid of rats, you must get rid of the garbage. If you have rats, you can poison them, trap them, shoot them or eliminate them in a variety of other ways. But if the garbage upon which they were feeding remains, more rats will be drawn to it.

Meditate on that for a few minutes. Pray about it and ask the Holy Spirit to show you how it may apply to your life, or even to your church. You may discover that there is something holding your present borders in place. It may not be sexual sin, addictions, severe anger, greed, pride or some other such unrighteous thing. It could be fear, or doubt, or unbelief that holds our borders of faith and expectation in place.

Chapter 18

The Purpose of Signs and Wonders

I pray that some of the signs and wonders shared in this book are encouraging to you. As you experience the wondrous works of God, you will not only increase your own faith and expectation, but you will become a source of encouragement to others.

My personal belief is that most non-believers do not really care what your theology or doctrine is; they want to know if God is real and whether or not He gets involved in people's lives in real ways.

A sign is something that points to or identifies or verifies something greater than itself. Signs and wonders point to the God we serve.

> And they went out and preached everywhere, while the Lord worked with them and confirmed the word by the signs that followed. (Mark 16:20)

> Men of Israel listen to these words: Jesus the Nazarene, a man attested to you by God with miracles and wonders and signs which God performed through Him in your midst... (Acts 2:22)

Attested means to certify, bear witness, show forth, or prove. Signs and wonders are to confirm or validate that God's Word is true—both the living Word and the written Word, as God has said.

Signs and wonders show forth the goodness and greatness of God to make His people whole. They manifest His love and power. They all point to Him. They confirm the Word of God. They show that God's Word works in those who believe, just as He has spoken. And all the glory and praise is to go to Him!

You have probably experienced signs, wonders, and miracles in your church and in your personal life. Again, the purpose of this book is to help us all realize that, no matter what our past experience has been, God has much, much more for all of us!

Let's try to work together to provided the environment or atmosphere that will allow Him to do even much more.

Signs and Wonders and Faith

The Scriptures give many accounts of Christ-followers performing signs and wonders. Here are only a few.

Everyone kept feeling a sense of awe; and many *wonders and signs* were taking place through the apostles. (Acts 2:43)

The word of God kept on spreading; and the number of the disciples continued to increase greatly in Jerusalem, and a great many of the priests were becoming obedient to the faith. And Stephen, full of grace and power, was performing great *wonders and signs* among the people. (Acts 6:7–8)

Therefore they spent a long time there speaking boldly, with reliance upon the Lord, who was testifying to the word of His grace, granting that *signs and wonders* be done by their hands. (Acts 14:3)

All the people kept silent, and they were listening to Barnabas and Paul as they were relating what *signs and wonders* God had done through them among the Gentiles. (Acts 15:12)

Signs That Follow Believers Who Walk In Faith

These signs will accompany those who have believed: in my name they will cast out demons, they will speak with new tongues, they will pick up serpents, and if they drink any deadly thing it will not hurt them; they will lay hands on the sick and they will recover. So then, when the Lord Jesus had spoken to them, He was received up into heaven and sat down at the right hand of God. And they went out and preached everywhere, while the Lord worked with them, and confirmed the word by the signs that followed. (Mark 16:17–20)

We often refer to the book that follows the four Gospels as the Book of Acts. More properly it should be The Acts of the Apostles. That spells out more clearly that this book is about the acts or deeds of the Christ-followers of that time after they had received the mighty Baptism in the Holy Spirit.

Note a common thread in the Scripture passages quoted above. Signs and wonders were *performed* by the believers, they occurred *at their hands*, but it was the Holy Spirit of God who was moving powerfully through them and making it all possible.

The verses from Mark are preceded by this: "Go into all the world and preach the Gospel to all creation" (Mark 16:15). The charge by Jesus was to preach the Gospel, preach the Kingdom, preach the Word of God; and if they would do so by faith, He would confirm or validate that Word with supernatural signs and wonders.

They spent time preaching the Word *with reliance on the Lord,* and the Lord was *testifying to that Word with signs and wonders.* As the believers preached the Word, signs accompanied them.

When they preached the Word of healing, the Lord healed people through them. As they preached forgiveness, the Lord convicted people of the need to forgive. As they preached deliverance, they cast out demons in accordance to the Word preached and the power of the Holy Spirit within them.

God's Confirmation of His Word

Signs and wonders are God's testimony or witness regarding His Word. He is showing how the Word works in those who believe. Signs and wonders verify or authenticate the Word as absolute and unchanging truth.

Paul said this to the believers at Rome:

> Therefore in Christ Jesus I have found reason for boasting in things pertaining to God. For I will not presume to speak of anything except what Christ has accomplished through me, resulting in the obedience of the Gentiles by word and deed, in the power of signs and wonders, in the power of the Spirit, so that from Jerusalem and round about as far as Illyricum I have fully preached the Gospel of Christ. (Romans 15:17–19)

Paul said he could boast in what the Lord had done through him because, as he preached the Gospel, he preached it fully. To fully preach the Gospel is to preach it in the power of the Holy Spirit with accompanying supernatural signs and wonders to confirm the Word proclaimed.

"....God also testifying with them, both by signs and wonders and by various miracles and gifts of the Holy Spirit according to His own will" (Hebrews 2:4). It is God's will that signs and wonders would be performed at the hands of believers who proclaim His Word with reliance on Him—in faith.

It is exciting to see how God moved through people in days gone by. It is even more exciting to read, "Jesus Christ is the same yesterday, and today, and forever" (Hebrews 13:8). You should expect signs and wonders to accompany the Word of God that you proclaim in faith!

It Continues On

He still performs signs and wonders today through *those who believe.*

Before empowering His followers, Jesus Himself performed many signs, wonders, and miracles. Lazarus was sick to the point of death. We read in John, Chapter eleven, that they sent for Jesus to come. He waited a few days before He went, and by the time He got there, Lazarus had died and had been buried in a tomb for four days.

Jesus called Lazarus out of death and out of the tomb. "Lazarus, come forth," He commanded. Then He told the people, "Unbind him, and let him go." But just before calling Lazarus forth, He said to those gathered there, "Did I not say to you that if you believe, you will see the glory of God?" (John 11:40).

Why did He say that? The same reason He said everything that He spoke, "...I do not speak on my own initiative, but by the Father abiding in Me" (John 14:10). Jesus said that He only spoke what He heard the Father speak. So in speaking to the people gathered at Lazarus' tomb, He was speaking the Word of God. Then God confirmed that Word by having Jesus call Lazarus forth.

God Reveals Himself Through Signs and Wonders

Signs and wonders encourage people to accept God's Word as truth. They display the integrity of His unchanging Word and unchanging character. It might be said that signs and wonders are God's signature verifying the authority of His Word.

It should be noted here that the signs that were to accompany the preaching of the Word were for "those who believe." When speaking of *preaching* the Word, it is not implied that one has to occupy a pulpit ministry or any other specific office of ministry. To preach simply means to proclaim. That applies to any believer who speaks the Word of God or shares the Word with others.

A key is that the Word is to be spoken in faith, believing what God has said. God's Word is a gift of grace that we receive by faith and speak forth with full assurance of things hoped for, evidence of what is not yet seen.

Signs and wonders are to be a part of believers' lives so they can draw others to Jesus and demonstrate how the Word of God manifests when it is received by faith.

Paul spoke to the believers at Corinth: "The signs of a true apostle were performed among you with all perseverance, by signs and wonders and miracles" (2 Corinthians 12:12).

Trusting in the Lord, relying on Him, and having faith in God's word will result in signs and wonders in *your* life as your faith is increasing. When signs occur, be sure to do what Paul did: boast in what the Lord is doing. Give Him all the glory! For it is "the word of God, which also performs its work in you who believe" (1 Thessalonians 2:13b).

"These signs will accompany those who have believed, in My name...."(Mark 16:17ff).

"Jesus Christ is the same yesterday and today and forever" (Hebrews 13:8).

Step out in faith, believing. Allow the Lord to use you as one of His instruments through which He can perform signs and wonders, bringing healing, deliverance, and wholeness to people as you share His Word in faith.

Chapter 19

Contending Earnestly for the Faith

The book of Jude was written by Jude, brother of James, half brother of Jesus, about sixty to eighty AD. His purpose in writing was to confront the problems of false teachers and false doctrine that were hindering, distorting, and destroying the believers' faith. Still even today his words are a reminder of the need for constant vigilance by believers not to compromise the Word of God or draw back from it.

> Beloved, while I was making every effort to write you about our common salvation, I felt the necessity to write to you appealing that you contend earnestly for the faith which was once for all handed down to the saints. (Jude 3)

Jude was exhorting the believers to fight for the faith which they had. Not just to fight for it, but to *earnestly* fight for it. Encouraging them to be faithful to Christ, he instructed them to hold on to what they had obtained and to hold on with intensity, tenacity, and purpose.

The Good Fight of Faith

Paul similarly wrote to the believers at Philippi:

> Only conduct yourselves in a manner worthy
> of the gospel of Christ, so that whether I
> come and see you or remain absent, I will
> hear of you that you are standing firm in one
> spirit, with one mind striving together for the
> faith of the gospel... (Philippians 1:27)

To contend is to stand firm and fight. Jude and Paul were encouraging believers to stand firm in faith. Stand firm on the unchangeable Word of God. Fight for truth. Defend the Lord and His Word.

> This command I entrust to you, Timothy,
> my son, in accordance with the prophecies
> previously made concerning you, that by
> them you fight the good fight, keeping faith
> and a good conscience, which some have
> rejected and suffered shipwreck in regard
> to their faith. (1 Timothy 1:18-19)

> Fight the good fight of faith... (1 Timothy
> 6:12a)

When you begin to develop your faith, a battle will ensue. There will be people and even circumstances that will speak out against the very Word of God which you have learned to receive by faith. To contend is literally to fight as a combatant. We are to exert ourselves to the utmost in defense of God's Word and our faith, even when it seems costly. It may mean taking a stand against those even in the churches who deny the authority of God's Word and who deny His power.

Faith Never Compromises

Above we read that Paul spoke of those who have rejected faith, or who had faith and it became shipwrecked.

> But the Spirit explicitly says that in later times some will fall away from the faith, paying attention to deceitful spirits and doctrines of demons... (1 Timothy 4:1)

Falling away implies they once had faith but lost it.

Walking in faith—living in faith—is not something that we begin and then just put on cruise control. We must carefully watch over our faith, develop it ever stronger, and steadfastly resist any effort to compromise, diminish, or destroy it.

We must contend earnestly for our faith. Those in faith must never allow God's Word to be compromised in its authority, or distorted in its truth, or explained away regarding its power and promises.

> But realize this, that in the last days difficult times will come. For men will be lovers of self, lovers of money, boastful, arrogant, revilers, disobedient to parents, ungrateful, unholy, unloving, irreconcilable, malicious gossips, without self-control, brutal, haters

of good, treacherous, reckless, conceited, lovers of pleasure rather than lovers of God, holding to a form of godliness, although they have denied its power. Avoid such men as these. (2 Timothy 3:1-5)

Isaiah prophesied long ago of these days:

Then the Lord said, "... this people draw near with their words and honor Me with their lip service, but they remove their hearts far from Me, and their reverence for Me consists of tradition learned by rote." (Isaiah 29:13)

Tradition Is Not the Basis for Faith

Jesus spoke to a group of just such people: the Pharisees and Scribes. "And He answered and said to them, 'Why do you yourselves transgress the commandment of God for the sake of your tradition?" (Matthew 15:3). Then He quoted Isaiah's prophecy:

You hypocrites, rightly did Isaiah prophesy of you: "This people honors Me with their lips, but their heart is far away from Me. But in vain do they worship Me, teaching as doctrines the precepts of men." (Matthew 15:7-9)

There are people today who go to church, hold to the traditions of their denomination, obey all the rules of the church, yet deny the truth and power of God's Word. They are not living by faith. You can not live by faith if you do not believe God's Word is true. You have no basis for your faith.

> All Scripture is inspired by God and profitable for teaching, for reproof, for correction, for training in righteousness; so that the man of God may be adequate, equipped for every good work. (2 Timothy 3:16)

"The grass withers, the flower fades, but the Word of our God stands forever" (Isaiah 40:8). The unchanging Word of God is the basis for our faith. Do not let others tell you differently.

We must contend for our faith without distorting it, without trying to adapt the Word to fit our circumstances. We are to adapt our circumstances to the Word of God.

As we have seen, Scripture clearly tells us that not all who start out in faith end in faith. Some will fall away; some will be shipwrecked in their faith. Some will lightly esteem their faith, thus rendering it ineffective.

Circumstances will cause some to compromise their faith, saying, "Well, so and so really loved God and was not healed, so God must just heal some, but not others. It must not be His will to heal everyone." Is that what the Word of God says?

Faith Does Not Shrink Back

> Jesus was going through all the cities and villages, teaching in their synagogues and proclaiming the gospel of the kingdom, and healing every kind of disease and every kind of sickness. (Matthew 9:35)

> Jesus Christ is the same yesterday and today and forever. (Hebrews 13:8)

We must not pull back in these days from proclaiming *all* of God's Word—as it is written. Do not add to His Word because of the sake of your tradition or what your friends might say that contradicts it. That is what Paul called "shrinking" back.

Paul said, "For I did not shrink from declaring to you the whole purpose of God" (Acts 20:27). Other versions say the *whole counsel* of God. We could say he did not hold back from preaching the whole Word of God.

Paul did not hold back by ceasing to preach the fullness of the Word of God even when faced with stiff opposition or circumstances that appeared contrary to the Word.

"Do not throw away your confidence, which has a great reward" (Hebrews 10:35). When your confidence is in the Lord and in His Word, you are in faith. Faith has a great reward.

What does God say about the one who draws back from faith? "But My righteous one shall live by faith, and if he shrinks back, My soul has no pleasure in him" (Hebrews 10:38). The writer of the book of Hebrews said, "But we are not of those who shrink back to destruction, but of those who have faith to the preserving of the soul" (Hebrews 10:39).

Stay Strong in Faith

As we contend earnestly with our enemies, the opponents of our faith, we must do so out of strength. We must keep strong in faith.

Jude again has some sound advice. "But you, beloved, building yourselves up on your most holy faith, praying in the Holy Spirit..." (Jude 20).

Stay in the fight. Contend earnestly for your faith. As you face opposition to your development of overcoming, mountain-moving faith, stand strong and press on! "For we have become partakers of Christ, if we hold fast the beginning of our assurance firm until the end... " (Hebrews 3:14).

Fear—The Great Enemy of Faith

> Those who are led by the Spirit of God are sons of God. For you did not receive a spirit of slavery leading to fear again, but you have received a spirit of adoption as sons by which we cry out, "Abba! Father." (Romans 8:14-15)

"For God has not given us a spirit of fear, but of power and love and discipline" (2 Timothy 1:7). Over and over in Scripture when God talks to His people He says, "Fear not. Be not afraid. Fret not. *Be not afraid.*"

God calls His people to faith, to believe in Him, that they might expect good things from Him.

Fear, if allowed to reign, will cancel our faith. One of the fears that limit some people is the fear of the unknown. What if we expand the borders of our expectations and something weird seems to happen? Be assured by His Word:

> O what man is there among you who, when his son asks for a loaf, will give him a stone? Or if he asks for a fish, he will not give him a snake, will he? If you then, being evil, know how to give good gifts to your children, how much more will your Father who is in heaven give what is good to those who ask Him! (Matthew 7:9-11)

If we ask God for His gifts or promises or provisions, He will help us to see to it that what we receive is from Him. Along with that assurance, we can use the gift of discernment of spirits as spoken of in 1st Corinthians 12:10.

There are two aspects of discerning or distinguishing the spirits behind something or present in someone. One, the Holy Spirit will bear witness with your spirit as to whether something you are witnessing is from God or not.

Second, you can judge by the character and fruit of what you are questioning. Does it line up with the Word of God? Does it line up with His character and nature?

As an example, a member of our church moved to another town and was checking out churches in that area. He called me one night with a question. He described a service he attended in which people were running around the sanctuary and banging their heads against the wall.

He said he turned to a nearby member of that church and asked what was going on. His answer was, "Oh, that's just the Holy Spirit at work. You know, when the Holy Spirit comes upon you, you just lose control!"

His question for me was, "Was that the Holy Spirit?" My short answer was, no. My explanation included that part of the fruit of the Spirit is *self-control*. See Galatians 5:22-23. Further, God's Spirit would not cause His beloved children to bang their heads on the wall and possibly get a concussion.

When we call on God for His love and power to be manifested in and through us, we need not fear. He will respond to our sincere desire to know and experience more of Him in ways *always* according to His Word and His character and nature.

Unneeded fear will hinder your efforts to expand your borders of faith and expectation.

Chapter 20

What Are You Expecting?

Once you decide that you personally want to expand the borders of your expectation and you want to be a part of helping your church do the same, you need to think about what it is you are expecting. Are there things in the Word of God that are promised or provided that you have not experienced? Is there a level of faith that you have not yet attained?

There are three elements of Bible faith: Believing, speaking, and acting according to what you believe and say. The three elements must all be in agreement. Bible faith, the kind of faith Christ-followers are to have, must be based on the Word of God.

We must *believe* what God's Word says, not adding to it. We must *declare* that Word, not adding to it. Then we must *act* in agreement with those two elements.

It is important to realize that the three elements will work for us, releasing or manifesting the provisions and promises of God, or they can work against us, having nothing to do with what God has for us.

An example: Well, the flu season is coming. I catch it every year, so I might as well stock up on the medications so I'll be ready for it when it comes. This statement, spoken out, is in agreement with what the speaker believes and expects. The one making the declaration is obviously expecting to catch the flu. He believes it, speaks it, then puts into action that which agrees with what he believes and says. And, guess what? The person will very likely get the flu!

You can probably think of similar statements you have made. Think about it for a few minutes. We need to believe and agree by speaking God's Word. Then *act* like we believe it.

Chapter 21

We Release the Power of the One We Agree With

You release the power of the one you agree with. Look at Romans 6:16 very carefully.

> Do you not know that when you present yourselves to someone as slaves for obedience, you are slaves of the one whom you obey, either of sin resulting in death, or of obedience resulting in righteousness?

If you submit to and agree with the devil and his underlings (demons), you release his power and his will into your life. When you submit to the Lord and agree with Him, you release the promises and provisions of God into your life.

The reason some Christians suffer is that they try to serve two masters, and the Bible says that just will not work. That is one reason we should take our every thought captive unto the obedience of Christ. See 2 Corinthians 10:5. We need to pay attention to our thoughts and ask ourselves whether or not they agree with God's Word.

If not, take the thought into captivity and ask yourself, If Jesus were right here in front of me bodily, would He say that to me? Immediately you will know.

May I say it once again. Expand your borders to include only that which agrees with God's Word. Continue to renew your mind to think in agreement with the Word of God according to Romans 12:2:

> And do not be conformed to this world, but be transformed by the renewing of your mind, so that you may prove what the will of God is, that which is good and acceptable and perfect.

Jesus said, "Therefore everyone who hears these words of Mine and acts on them may be compared to a wise man who built his house on a rock" (Matthew 7:24).

Fear Not the Supernatural

Supernatural is defined as existing or occurring outside the normal experience or knowledge of man.

Some may fear the supernatural because of an unbalanced view they have been taught, or they may have seen movies about bizarre, even terrorizing things that are viewed as supernatural. The conclusion, then, may be that anything that does not fit in with natural laws of biology or physics can not be good.

On the other hand, Jesus walking on water; the feeding of five thousand plus people with five small fish and some crackers; healing lepers, deaf people, blind people, lame people, and people who could not speak are all good things, and they involve the supernatural. And wasn't casting a legion of demons out of a man who was completely out of control a good thing?

Jesus said clearly that those who believe and follow Him should do the same works that He did: proclaim the Kingdom of God, heal the sick, and cast out demons. Doing these things involves the supernatural. Therefore, the supernatural gifts or manifestations of God are not to be avoided or feared, but rather should be earnestly desired and sought.

In John 14:12 Jesus said it this way: "Truly, truly, I say to you, he who believes in Me, the works that I do, he will do also; and greater works than these he will do; because I go to the Father." Doing the works of Jesus by the power of the Holy Spirit involves the supernatural. It is not natural power. They are not natural works. Do not fear, but embrace the supernatural as long as it lines up with and is consistent with the Word of God.

Yes, the demonic powers of darkness at times operate outside the natural realm, but we have already seen that we have authority over them.

> Behold, I have given you authority to tread on serpents and scorpions, and over all the power of the enemy... (Luke 10:19)

> These signs will accompany those who believe: in my name they will cast out

demons, they will speak with new tongues; they will pick up serpents, and if they drink any deadly thing it will not hurt them; they will lay hands on the sick, and they will recover. (Mark 16:17-18)

These are supernatural signs that are to accompany *believers.*

Chapter 22

The Sin of Unbelief

Sin is defined in the Greek language of the New Testament as "missing the mark." It is said to be a term used in archery when the arrow misses its target. Sin does not mean the person who sins is a bad, nasty person. It means the person has missed God's Word by not believing it and following it.

Man ranks sin. Lying, greed, or pride may not seem to be very bad sins. Murder, robbery, or rape seem like horrible sins. God does not rank them as man does. Any sin is missing the mark of God's Word, as the arrow misses the target. Some might not think of unbelief as a sin. Not believing God's Word is about as far off of hitting the target as you can get. Unbelief is the complete opposite of belief.

> Take care, brethren, that there not be in any one of you an evil, unbelieving heart that falls away from the living God. (Hebrews 3:12)

> For indeed we have had the good news preached to us, just as they also; but the word they heard did not profit them, because it was not united by faith in those who heard. (Hebrews 4:2)

Unbelief and lack of expectation prevent God's power from flowing into us and through us. If it hindered Jesus in His ministry, it will hinder us, also.

> And He did not do many miracles there because of their unbelief. (Matthew 13:58).

> And He could do no miracles there except that He laid His hands on a few sick people and healed them. And He wondered at their unbelief. (Mark 6:5-6)

Your faith and expectation must be based on God's Word, which is never changing. "Faith comes from hearing, and hearing from the word of God" (Romans 10:17).

Faith comes forth out of your spirit as the Holy Spirit reveals the truth and power in God's Word. We have the true belief, the assurance, that the promises of God are real.

> Now faith is the assurance of things hoped for, the conviction of things not seen. (Hebrews 11:1)

> The grass withers, the flower fades, but the word of our God stands forever. (Isaiah 40:8)

Chapter 23

Asking God to Do What He Has Empowered Us to Do

In reading and learning from the Scripture, we must read it all. We saw earlier according to Proverbs 30:5–6 that we are not to add to God's Word. We are also not to subtract from it. Have you ever heard someone say to a person who is struggling with something in his life, "God causes all things to work together for good?" They use that as encouragement, but it is not what the Bible says.

Look at the verse in its entirety: "And we know that God causes all things to work together for good to those who love God, *to those who are called according to His purpose*" (Romans 8:28).

Do not add to, nor subtract from what the Scriptures say. This passage is not for everyone. It is for those who love God and are called according to His purpose and are following after their calling.

Maybe you have told someone who feels bound by something in his life, "Well, the Bible says that the truth shall set you free!" You would be referring to John 8:31–32. Or rather a part of the passage. In it's entirety it reads as follows: "*If you continue in My word, then you are truly disciples of Mine;* and you will know the truth, and the truth will make you free."

Jesus is saying that, if a person abides in and continues to learn from His Word, He will become a disciple of His who will come to know the truth of God's Word and be set free. Do not add to, nor subtract from, the Word of God.

This is important enough to give one more example. Some Christians get really excited when they read or hear the passage that says, "Now to Him who is able to do far more abundantly beyond all that we ask or think, to Him be the glory in the church and in Christ Jesus to all generations forever and ever. Amen."

Missing is the part that says, "according to the power that works within us" (Ephesians 3:20–21). God's exceeding abundant works are in accord with the power that works within us. "According to" means in harmony with or in agreement with. It also carries the implication of being directly proportional to.

Why is this so important? As a student, can you imagine that you would ask your teacher to do your homework and class projects for you? Can you imagine a football player asking his coach to go onto the field and run the plays for him? God has given us power and authority to do certain things, and we should not be asking Him to do what He has already asked us to do.

We have seen that we are to proclaim the Gospel, heal the sick, and cast out demons. As you continue to expand the borders of your faith and expectation, be sure that all is based on God's Word—as it is written, no more, no less. And as you press on, do not expect Him to do what He has equipped and called you to do, either as an individual or as a church.

Chapter 24

Avoiding Pride at All Costs

Pride can be defined as arrogance or haughtiness. It is self-centeredness. Giving accolades to oneself. Pride is taking the praise and glory that belongs to God. The book of Proverbs has several things to say about pride.

> When pride comes, then comes dishonor. But with the humble is wisdom. (Proverbs 11:2)

> A man's pride will bring him low, but a humble spirit will obtain honor. (Proverbs 29:23)

> Pride goes before destruction and a haughty spirit before stumbling. (Proverbs 16:18)

As you expand your borders of faith and expectation, God is able to do more in you and through you, in your church and through your church. Always remember— never forget—Jesus' words, "I am the vine, you are the branches; he who abides in Me, and I in Him, he bears much fruit; for apart from Me you can do nothing" (John 15:5).

We can do nothing without Him. As He moves in and through you to accomplish wondrous things, always be sure you give all the glory to Him; for apart from Him you could not have done it or experienced it. At the same time, the following phrase is used several times in the Bible that, "With God all things are possible."

When you lay hands on the sick and they are healed, or if you cast demons out and the person is set free, who is doing it? You, or Jesus? The answer is, yes. You can not do it by yourself, and He has chosen to work through you. You are partners in it. You are working with God, and with God "All things are possible to him who believes" (Mark 9:23).

It is a great joy to participate with God in His wondrous works, but all the credit, all the praise, all the glory goes to Him. He *could* do it without us, but we could not do it without Him.

The Word of God says we are partners, companions, sharers with Him. The word "partaker" means those things in the Scripture below. What a privilege it is to partner with Him!

> For by these He has granted to us His precious and magnificent promises, in order that by them you might become partakers of the divine nature, having escaped the corruption that is in the world by lust. (2 Peter 1:4)

Chapter 25

The Power of Our Testimony

As you continue to expand your borders of faith and expectation, you will increasingly experience wondrous things from God. Do not hesitate to share your testimony with others in a loving and non-prideful way. Let others be encouraged that they, too, may want to expand their own borders.

Why is it that most Christians do not hesitate to tell others about a new restaurant they found to be good, a book they found interesting, or even about a new recipe they tried, yet they are hesitant to tell others about some amazing things that God is doing in their lives?

Don't you admire the boldness and courage of the disciples Peter and John when they responded to those who were persecuting them and telling them to stop speaking about Jesus? They replied, "We can not stop speaking about what we have seen and heard" (Acts 4:20).

Then they prayed with their friends, "And now, Lord, take note of their threats and grant that your bond-servants may speak Your word with all confidence, while You extend Your hand to heal, and signs and wonders take place through the name of Your holy servant Jesus" (Acts 4:29–30).

God's response to their bold prayer: "And when they had prayed, the place where they had gathered together was shaken, and they were all filled with the Holy Spirit and began to speak the word of God with boldness" (Acts 4:31).

Do you suppose that, if your church took a stand and prayed that way, they might get a similar response from God?

Chapter 26

The Importance of Praying in Faith

"The effective prayer of a righteous man can accomplish much" (James 5:16).

"Devote yourselves to prayer, keeping alert in it with an attitude of thanksgiving" (Colossians 4:2).

Devoting yourself to prayer will be an important part of expanding your borders of faith and expectation. Part of that devotion to prayer includes keeping alert in it. This does not mean just staying awake while you pray. It means that if we are praying with faith and expectancy, we realize prayer is not just talking *to* God, it is talking *with* God.

Our prayers should include standing firm in faith in God's Word, declaring His Word, and claiming or laying hold of His promises. The words we speak in prayer must be in agreement with God's Word to be effective. Remember, you release the power of the one you agree with! An effective prayer is one filled with energy, passion, faith, and expectation.

Prayer was not meant to be a proverbial laundry list of things we want, or desire, or think we need. God knows our needs. Our prayers should be filled with worship, praise, and thanksgiving for who He is and for all He has promised us.

One of the principle things we need to be alert to hear from Him is wisdom. "Wisdom is the principle thing" (Proverbs 4:7).

> If any of you lack wisdom, let him ask of God, who gives to all men generously and without reproach, and it will be given to him. But let him ask in faith without any doubting, for the one who doubts is like the surf of the sea, driven and tossed by the wind. (James 1:5–6)

"Pray without ceasing" (1 Thessalonians 5:17). Obviously that does not mean that you spend every minute of every day in prayer. Rather, it means that we pray consistently.

You do not have to get legalistic about it, thinking you *must* pray at a certain time each day or for a certain length of time. You may want to set aside certain times just to pray for the discipline of it. But don't you think we can pray throughout the day, talking to and listening to God?

I wonder how long a marriage would last if the husband told his wife, I am going to be a really faithful husband. I will talk with you for thirty minutes every day from 2:00 to 2:30 p.m. That would not be a very intimate relationship.

God wants an intimate relationship with us in which we can communicate *with* each other throughout the day.

This is in no way meant to be a complete teaching on prayer. These thoughts are to encourage you to expand your borders regarding what you might expect in prayer.

Chapter 27

Leaving a Legacy of Faith

Legacy = Something that has been handed down from an ancestor or predecessor. Our legacy is what we leave behind for those who follow after us. We often think of legacy as something we leave for our children upon our death—an inheritance. It is often thought of in terms of material possessions alone.

Some people work hard all their lives to accumulate wealth so they can leave behind houses, cars, stocks, investments, and whatever will make life easier for their children after they themselves are gone. There is nothing wrong with wanting to bless your children. But there is something greater than material possessions: a legacy of faith and expectation. By instruction and example we can leave our children a greater understanding of faith than what we may have inherited.

We can also leave a legacy of faith and expectation to those beyond our own family, and the legacy can enter into effect even before we die. As others see your integrity and passion for true overcoming, mountain-moving faith, it may draw them to a like desire to bring glory to God and to please Him with real biblical faith. As they see you expanding your borders of expectation, they will be encouraged to do the same.

As they see that you know what the promises and provisions of God are, and they see you receiving them into your life, they will see how faith and the Word of God work in and through human flesh. They will see that biblical faith is not just a philosophy or theory. It is a reality that God created.

As others see steadfastness and consistency in your reliance on the Word of God and in your confidence in the Lord, they may be encouraged to imitate those who by faith and patience inherit the promises" (Hebrews 6:12).

Leaving a legacy of faith for others is far more valuable than whatever material possessions you may accumulate and leave behind.

May the Lord bless your endeavors to illustrate to others what faith is, so they may see and understand that, "Without faith it is impossible to please Him, for he who comes to God must believe that He is and that He is a rewarder of those who seek Him" (Hebrews 11:6).

"Let us hold fast the confession of our hope without wavering, for He who promised is faithful" (Hebrews 10:23).

"Now may the God of hope fill you with all joy and peace in believing, so that you will abound in hope by the power of the Holy Spirit" (Romans 15:13).

Chapter 28

Where Do We Go From Here?

Have you received any encouragement from reading this book? Are you ready to expand the borders of your faith and expectation? Are you ready to remove the limitations you have placed on God? Are you ready to start where you are and press on to learn more about, and experience more of, the wondrous works of God?

If so, let us all give the praise and glory to God and look forward to new and great things in your life and in your church.

Most of us were not raised in homes where strong biblical faith was encouraged since infanthood. Some spent many years before coming to the place they really learned and believed God's Word. But if you are now ready to expand, go for it. Expand the borders of your expectation. God has more for you!

Printed in the United States
By Bookmasters